Great Works

Instructional Guides for Literature

In the Year of the Boar and Jackie Robinson

A guide for the novel by Bette Bao Lord
Great Works Author: Chandra C. Prough, M.S.Ed., NBCT

SHELL EDUCATION

Publishing Credits

Corinne Burton, M.A.Ed., *President*; Conni Medina, M.A.Ed., *Managing Editor*; Emily R. Smith, M.A.Ed., *Content Director*; Lee Aucoin, *Senior Graphic Designer*; Stephanie Bernard, *Assistant Editor*; Don Tran, *Graphic Designer*

Image Credits

Cover page photo Bob Sandberg/LOC [LC-DIG-ppmsc-00048]; all other cover images iStock

Standards

© 2007 Teachers of English to Speakers of Other Languages, Inc. (TESOL)
© 2007 Board of Regents of the University of Wisconsin System. World-Class Instructional Design and Assessment (WIDA)
© Copyright 2010. National Governors Association Center for Best Practices and Council of Chief State School Officers. All rights reserved.
© Copyright 2007–2015. Texas Education Association (TEA). All rights reserved.

Shell Education

A division of Teacher Created Materials
5301 Oceanus Drive
Huntington Beach, CA 92649-1030
ISBN 978-1-4258-1719-0
https://www.tcmpub.com/shell-education
© 2017 Shell Educational Publishing, Inc.

Table of Contents

How to Use This Literature Guide

Today's standards demand rigor and relevance in the reading of complex texts. The units in this series guide teachers in a rich and deep exploration of worthwhile works of literature for classroom study. The most rigorous instruction can also be interesting and engaging!

Many current strategies for effective literacy instruction have been incorporated into these instructional guides for literature. Throughout the units, text-dependent questions are used to determine comprehension of the book as well as student interpretation of the vocabulary words. The books chosen for the series are complex exemplars of carefully crafted works of literature. Close reading is used throughout the units to guide students toward revisiting the text and using textual evidence to respond to prompts orally and in writing. Students must analyze the story elements in multiple assignments for each section of the book. All of these strategies work together to rigorously guide students through their study of literature.

The next few pages will make clear how to use this guide for a purposeful and meaningful literature study. Each section of this guide is set up in the same way to make it easier for you to implement the instruction in your classroom.

Theme Thoughts

The great works of literature used throughout this series have important themes that have been relevant to people for many years. Many of the themes will be discussed during the various sections of this instructional guide. However, it would also benefit students to have independent time to think about the key themes of the novel.

Before students begin reading, have them complete *Pre-Reading Theme Thoughts* (page 13). This graphic organizer will allow students to think about the themes outside the context of the story. They'll have the opportunity to evaluate statements based on important themes and defend their opinions. Be sure to have students keep their papers for comparison to the *Post-Reading Theme Thoughts* (page 59). This graphic organizer is similar to the pre-reading activity. However, this time, students will be answering the questions from the point of view of one of the characters in the novel. They have to think about how the character would feel about each statement and defend their thoughts. To conclude the activity, have students compare what they thought about the themes before they read the novel to what the characters discovered during the story.

How to Use This Literature Guide *(cont.)*

Vocabulary

Each teacher reference vocabulary overview page has definitions and sentences about how key vocabulary words are used in the section. These words should be introduced and discussed with students. Students will use these words in different activities throughout the book.

On some of the vocabulary student pages, students are asked to answer text-related questions about vocabulary words from the sections. The following question stems will help you create your own vocabulary questions if you'd like to extend the discussion.

- How does this word describe _____'s character?
- How does this word connect to the problem in this story?
- How does this word help you understand the setting?
- Tell me how this word connects to the main idea of this story.
- What visual pictures does this word bring to your mind?
- Why do you think the author used this word?

At times, you may find that more work with the words will help students understand their meanings and importance. These quick vocabulary activities are a good way to further study the words.

- Students can play vocabulary concentration. Make one set of cards that has the words on them and another set with the definitions. Then, have students lay them out on the table and play concentration. The goal of the game is to match vocabulary words with their definitions. For early readers or English language learners, the two sets of cards could be the words and pictures of the words.

- Students can create word journal entries about the words. Students choose words they think are important and then describe why they think each word is important within the book. Early readers or English language learners could instead draw pictures about the words in a journal.

- Students can create puppets and use them to act out the vocabulary words from the stories. Students may also enjoy telling their own character-driven stories using vocabulary words from the original stories.

How to Use This Literature Guide (cont.)

Analyzing the Literature

After you have read each section with students, hold a small-group or whole-class discussion. Provided on the teacher reference page for each section are leveled questions. The questions are written at two levels of complexity to allow you to decide which questions best meet the needs of your students. The Level 1 questions are typically less abstract than the Level 2 questions. These questions are focused on the various story elements, such as character, setting, and plot. Be sure to add further questions as your students discuss what they've read. For each question, a few key points are provided for your reference as you discuss the book with students.

Reader Response

In today's classrooms, there are often great readers who are below average writers. So much time and energy is spent in classrooms getting students to read on grade level that little time is left to focus on writing skills. To help teachers include more writing in their daily literacy instruction, each section of this guide has a literature-based reader response prompt. Each of the three genres of writing is used in the reader responses within this guide: narrative, informative/explanatory, and opinion. Before students write, you may want to allow them time to draw pictures related to the topic.

Guided Close Reading

Within each section of this guide, it is suggested that you closely reread a portion of the text with your students. Page numbers are given, but since some versions of the books may have different page numbers, the sections to be reread are described by location as well. After rereading the section, there are a few text-dependent questions to be answered by students.

Working space has been provided to help students prepare for the group discussion. They should record their thoughts and ideas on the activity page and refer to it during your discussion. Rather than just taking notes, you may want to require students to write complete responses to the questions before discussing them with you.

Encourage students to read one question at a time and then go back to the text and discover the answer. Work with students to ensure that they use the text to determine their answers rather than making unsupported inferences. Suggested answers are provided in the answer key.

How to Use This Literature Guide (cont.)

Guided Close Reading (cont.)

The generic open-ended stems below can be used to write your own text-dependent questions if you would like to give students more practice.

- What words in the story support . . . ?
- What text helps you understand . . . ?
- Use the book to tell why _____ happens.
- Based on the events in the story, . . . ?
- Show me the part in the text that supports . . . .
- Use the text to tell why . . . .

Making Connections

The activities in this section help students make cross-curricular connections to mathematics, science, social studies, fine arts, or other curricular areas. These activities require higher-order thinking skills from students but also allow for creative thinking.

Language Learning

A special section has been set aside to connect the literature to language conventions. Through these activities, students will have opportunities to practice the conventions of standard English grammar, usage, capitalization, and punctuation.

Story Elements

It is important to spend time discussing what the common story elements are in literature. Understanding the characters, setting, plot, and theme can increase students' comprehension and appreciation of the story. If teachers begin discussing these elements in early childhood, students will more likely internalize the concepts and look for the elements in their independent reading. Another very important reason for focusing on the story elements is that students will be better writers if they think about how the stories they read are constructed.

In the story elements activities, students are asked to create work related to the characters, setting, or plot. Consider having students complete only one of these activities. If you give students a choice on this assignment, each student can decide to complete the activity that most appeals to him or her. Different intelligences are used so that the activities are diverse and interesting to all students.

How to Use This Literature Guide (cont.)

Culminating Activity

This open-ended, cross-curricular activity requires higher-order thinking and allows for a creative product. Students will enjoy getting the chance to share what they have discovered through reading the novel. Be sure to allow them enough time to complete the activity at school or home.

Comprehension Assessment

The questions in this section are modeled after current standardized tests to help students analyze what they've read and prepare for tests they may see in their classrooms. The questions are dependent on the text and require critical-thinking skills to answer.

Response to Literature

The final post-reading activity is an essay based on the text that also requires further research by students. This is a great way to extend this book into other curricular areas. A suggested rubric is provided for teacher reference.

Correlation to the Standards

Shell Education is committed to producing educational materials that are research and standards based. As part of this effort, we have correlated all of our products to the academic standards of all 50 states, the District of Columbia, the Department of Defense Dependents Schools, and all Canadian provinces.

Purpose and Intent of Standards

The Every Student Succeeds Act (ESSA) mandates that all states adopt challenging academic standards that help students meet the goal of college and career readiness. While many states already adopted academic standards prior to ESSA, the act continues to hold states accountable for detailed and comprehensive standards. Standards are statements that describe the criteria necessary for students to meet specific academic goals. They define the knowledge, skills, and content students should acquire at each level. State standards are used in the development of our products, so educators can be assured they meet state academic requirements.

How to Find Standards Correlations

To print a customized correlation report of this product for your state, visit our website at **www.teachercreatedmaterials.com/administrators/correlations/** and follow the online directions. If you require assistance in printing correlation reports, please contact our Customer Service Department at 1-877-777-3450.

Correlation to the Standards (cont.)

Standards Correlation Chart

The lessons in this guide were written to support today's college and career readiness standards. This chart indicates which sections of this guide address which standards.

College and Career Readiness Standard	Section
Read closely to determine what the text says explicitly and to make logical inferences from it; cite specific textual evidence when writing or speaking to support conclusions drawn from the text.	Guided Close Reading Sections 1–5; Story Elements Sections 1–5; Making Connections Sections 3–4; Post-Reading Response to Literature
Determine central ideas or themes of a text and analyze their development; summarize the key supporting details and ideas.	Analyzing Literature Sections 1–5; Making Connections Sections 3, 5; Post-Reading Theme Thoughts
Analyze how and why individuals, events, or ideas develop and interact over the course of a text.	Analyzing Literature Sections 1–5; Story Elements Sections 1–5; Post-Reading Response to Literature
Interpret words and phrases as they are used in a text, including determining technical, connotative, and figurative meanings, and analyze how specific word choices shape meaning or tone.	Vocabulary Sections 1–5; Language Learning Section 1; Making Connections Sections 3–5
Analyze the structure of texts, including how specific sentences, paragraphs, and larger portions of the text (e.g., a section, chapter, scene, or stanza) relate to each other and the whole.	Guided Close Reading Sections 1–5
Assess how point of view or purpose shapes the content and style of a text.	Story Elements Section 5
Integrate and evaluate content presented in diverse media and formats, including visually and quantitatively, as well as in words.	Culminating Activity
Analyze how two or more texts address similar themes or topics in order to build knowledge or to compare the approaches the authors take.	Making Connections Section 4
Read and comprehend complex literary and informational texts independently and proficiently.	Entire Unit
Write arguments to support claims in an analysis of substantive topics or texts using valid reasoning and relevant and sufficient evidence.	Reader Response Sections 1, 3
Write informative/explanatory texts to examine and convey complex ideas and information clearly and accurately through the effective selection, organization, and analysis of content.	Reader Response Section 5; Story Elements Sections 1–5
Write narratives to develop real or imagined experiences or events using effective technique, well-chosen details and well-structured event sequences.	Reading Response Sections 2, 4
Produce clear and coherent writing in which the development, organization, and style are appropriate to task, purpose, and audience.	Pre-Reading Theme Thoughts; Guided Close Reading Sections 1–5, Post-Reading Response to Literature; Post–Reading Theme Thoughts
Use technology, including the Internet, to produce and publish writing and to interact and collaborate with others.	Culminating Activity; Making Connections Section 1

Standards Correlation Chart *(cont.)*

College and Career Readiness Standard	Section
Conduct short as well as more sustained research projects based on focused questions, demonstrating understanding of the subject under investigation.	Culminating Activity; Making Connections Section 1
Integrate and evaluate information presented in diverse media and formats, including visually, quantitatively, and orally.	Culminating Activity
Evaluate a speaker's point of view, reasoning, and use of evidence and rhetoric.	Story Elements Section 5
Present information, findings, and supporting evidence such that listeners can follow the line of reasoning and the organization, development, and style are appropriate to task, purpose, and audience.	Culminating Activity; Story Elements Section 4
Make strategic use of digital media and visual displays of data to express information and enhance understanding of presentations.	Culminating Activity
Adapt speech to a variety of contexts and communicative tasks, demonstrating command of formal English when indicated or appropriate.	Culminating Activity
Demonstrate command of the conventions of standard English grammar and usage when writing or speaking.	Culminating Activity; Reader Response Sections 1–5; Story Elements Sections 1–5
Demonstrate command of the conventions of standard English capitalization, punctuation, and spelling when writing.	Reader Response Sections 1–5; Story Elements Sections 1–5
Apply knowledge of language to understand how language functions in different contexts, to make effective choices for meaning or style, and to comprehend more fully when reading or listening.	Vocabulary Sections 1–5; Language Learning Section 4
Determine or clarify the meaning of unknown and multiple-meaning words and phrases by using context clues, analyzing meaningful word parts, and consulting general and specialized reference materials, as appropriate.	Vocabulary Sections 1–5; Language Learning Section 4
Demonstrate understanding of figurative language, word relationships, and nuances in word meanings.	Language Learning Sections 1–5
Acquire and use accurately a range of general academic and domain-specific words and phrases sufficient for reading, writing, speaking, and listening at the college and career readiness level; demonstrate independence in gathering vocabulary knowledge when encountering an unknown term important to comprehension or expression.	Vocabulary Sections 1–5

TESOL and WIDA Standards

The lessons in this book promote English language development for English language learners. The following TESOL and WIDA English Language Development Standards are addressed through the activities in this book:

- Standard 1: English language learners communicate for social and instructional purposes within the school setting.
- Standard 2: English language learners communicate information, ideas and concepts necessary for academic success in the content area of language arts.

About the Author–Bette Bao Lord

Bette Bao Lord was born in Shanghai, China, in 1938. Her father, Sandys Bao, came to live and work in New York in 1946 and later sent for his family, including Bette who was eight years old. Her infant sister, Sansun, was left behind with relatives and did not immigrate to the United States until 1962.

Through her experiences in public schools in both Brooklyn and New Jersey, Lord gained acceptance with her classmates and learned English by listening to baseball. She later went on to earn a bachelor's degree in political science at Tufts University in 1959 and a master's degree in law and diplomacy in 1960. She worked at the East-West Center in Hawaii and with the Fulbright Program for professors in Washington, D.C.

Lord based the novel *In the Year of the Boar and Jackie Robinson* on her experiences as a childhood immigrant in Brooklyn, New York. She credits her parents with making the experience a happy one because they taught her that she did not have to choose between the two cultures but could harmonize them. They told her, "You can be both [American and Chinese] and you can decide which part of each culture is right for you, that you want to believe in." (*Humanities*, November/December 2005, Volume 26/Number 6)

Prior to writing *In the Year of the Boar and Jackie Robinson*, her only novel for children, Lord won the American Book Award for *Spring Moon* (1981). The novel takes place in pre-revolutionary China through President Richard Nixon's visit in 1972. In her book *Middle Heart* (1996), she wrote about the early years of modern Chinese history ending with the student-led demonstrations in 1989. Later, Lord also wrote a book about her youngest sister's life in China and her escape *Eighth Moon: The True Story of a Young Girl's Life in Communist China* (2013).

Lord has been given many awards for her work as an author and democracy advocate, including the United States Information Agency Award for Outstanding Contributions. In 1998, President Bill Clinton presented her with the Eleanor Roosevelt Award for Human Rights.

Possible Texts for Text Comparisons

Since *In the Year of the Boar and Jackie Robinson* can be compared to books about the Chinese immigrant experience, good comparison texts include novels by Andrea Cheng. Her The Year of ... series follows an eight-year-old girl, Anna Wang, as she balances life between her American friends and her Chinese family.

Book Summary of *In the Year of the Boar and Jackie Robinson*

When Shirley Temple Wong is ten years old, she and her mother travel from China to Brooklyn, New York to join her father who has immigrated to the United States for work. Shirley's adjustment from her ancestral home in China to her parents' apartment in Brooklyn is full of fun and humorous situations. Shirley has to navigate the neighborhood, make new friends, as well as adjust to a new school and language.
At first, she has a difficult time connecting with other students because she is small, doesn't speak much English, and doesn't have good athletic skills. It isn't until she shows her unwavering loyalty to another fifth grader that she learns how to skate and play baseball. The newfound friendships and her love of baseball help Shirley to adjust to her new home while maintaining cultural traditions and connections to family in China.

Cross-Curricular Connection

This book can be used in a social science unit on China, New York City, friendship, immigration, civil rights, or cultural traditions.

Possible Texts for Text Sets

- Cheng, Andrea. 2015. *The Year of the Fortune Cookie.* HMH Books for Young Readers.
- ———. 2016. *The Year of the Three Sisters.* HMH Books for Young Readers.
- Herman, Gail. 2010. *Who Was Jackie Robinson?* Grosset & Dunlap.
- Robinson, Sharon. 2016. *The Hero Two Doors Down.* Scholastic Press.
- Shang, Wendy Wan-Long. 2013. *The Great Wall of Lucy Wu.* Scholastic Paperbacks.

Pre-Reading Theme Thoughts

Directions: Draw a picture of a happy face or a sad face. Your face should show how you feel about each statement. Then, use words to say what you think about each statement.

Statement	How Do You Feel? 😊 😦	Explain Your Answer
It is easy to make new friends.		
Learning new things is easy.		
It is important to tell an adult if someone hurts you.		
Good experiences can be bad, and bad experiences can turn out good.		

Teacher Plans

Vocabulary Overview

Key words and phrases from this section are provided below with definitions and sentences about how the words are used in the story. Introduce and discuss these important vocabulary words with students. If you think these words or other words in the story warrant more time devoted to them, there are suggestions in the introduction for other vocabulary activities (page 5).

Word	Definition	Sentence about Text
patriarch	oldest male member of a group or family	Bandit's **patriarch**, her grandfather, lets her pick her own American name even though she is a child.
scowled	made a frowning expression of displeasure	Bandit **scowls** at her cousin because she doesn't agree.
brazier	a pan for holding burning coals	The room grows cold as the coals in the **brazier** burn out.
harmony	pleasing or suitable arrangement of parts; agreement; accord	Grandmother believes that everything should be in **harmony** to welcome the new year.
summoned	called or sent for in order to meet	Grandmother **summons** Bandit to her quarters because she has something to tell her.
abacus	an instrument for making calculations by sliding beads along rods or in groves	Uncle uses the **abacus** beads to figure out his accounts.
mourners	people displaying signs of grief or sorrow for a death	The family cries like **mourners** because Bandit and her mother decide to move to America.
relented	became less severe, harsh, or strict	Grand-grand Aunt has never **relented** or forgiven her husband for making fun of her.
clan	a group of persons united by a common interest or ancestor	Bandit's grandfather is the head of the Bao family **clan**.
delicacies	something to eat that is rare or luxurious	Servants circle the floor with drinks and **delicacies**.

Vocabulary Activity

Directions: Choose four words that you feel are the most important in understanding the chapter. Write each word in a box below. Under each word, draw a picture to help you remember and understand the meaning of the word as it is used in the text.

Words from the Story

patriarch	scowled	brazier	harmony	summoned
abacus	mourners	relented	clan	delicacies

Word: _____

Word: _____

Word: _____

Word: _____

Analyzing the Literature

Provided below are discussion questions you can use in small groups, with the whole class, or for written assignments. Each question is written at two levels so that you can choose the right question for each group of students. For each question, a few key points are provided for your reference as you discuss the book with students.

Story Element	Level 1	Level 2	Key Discussion Points
Character	What do you know about Bandit's character?	How is Bandit similar to and different from other members of her family?	Bandit is an eight-year-old Chinese girl. She lives with her extended family and misses her father, who lives overseas. She gets along with both her grand-grand uncle and grand-grand aunt and acts as an intermediary. She has gotten in trouble with her grandmother for breaking things and is fearful of both her grandmother and her grandfather. She is not scared about moving to America unlike her other relatives, because she trusts her father and can't wait to see him.
Plot	What is the secret from Father's letter that makes Grandmother cry and Grandfather angry?	Why is the secret from Father's letter kept from Bandit, and why can't she ask what the secret is?	The secret is that Bandit and her mother are moving to America. Bandit isn't involved in the conversation when the letter is opened because she is a child and isn't allowed to question the conduct of the elders.
Setting	What is the setting of the chapter called "January"?	Describe the setting in "January." How does the setting influence your understanding of what is happening?	The setting is Bandit's family home in China during the 1940s. It is a large compound where the entire extended family lives, works, and raises their children. Bandit is one of many cousins who live there. The family is wealthy and has many servants. Everyone is under the watchful rule of Grandfather and Grandmother.

Reader Response

Think

Think about what you would do if you were told you and your family were going to move halfway around the world. Would you want to go?

Opinion Writing Prompt

Explain whether you would want to move. Give detailed reasons to support your decision.

_____

_____

_____

_____

_____

_____

_____

_____

_____

_____

_____

Guided Close Reading

Closely reread the section that starts with, "I was wondering about your freckles . . . ." Continue until, "Who asked *you*?"

Directions: Think about these questions. In the space below, write ideas as you think about the answers. Be ready to share your answers.

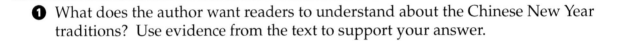

❶ What does the author want readers to understand about the Chinese New Year traditions? Use evidence from the text to support your answer.

❷ How does Bandit react when called up by her grandfather? What does this tell you about their relationship?

❸ What is the purpose of the details about the relationship between Grand-grand Uncle and his wife?

Making Connections-Naming Customs

Directions: Naming customs vary among cultures, families, and traditions. Use books or the Internet to look up naming customs from a culture or country other than your own. Then, find out about how and why you were given your name. Write at least three notes about each in the chart.

Culture Researched	My Name
_____	_____
Interesting facts about their naming customs:	Interesting facts about how I got my name:

Name _____ Date _____

Language Learning–Figurative Language

Directions: Whenever you describe something by comparing it with something else, you are using figurative language. Figurative language creates pictures for readers to imagine. Read the sentences below from the book. Then, circle the two ideas that are being compared in each sentence.

Language Hints!

- A simile is one type of figurative language.
- A simile is a comparison using the words *like* or *as*.

1. "Precious Coins was sitting on his bed .... She could not resist giving him a big hug. He was as cute as a dumpling and just as round."

2. "The lofty Hall of Ancestors was festooned with holiday banners and graced with clansmen from near and far. They formed clusters of color like the glass pieces in a kaleidoscope."

3. "Bandit felt that her face was as red as a fried lobster."

Directions: Look through this chapter of the book and find two more examples of similes. Write the sentences you find below.

4. _____

_____

5. _____

_____

Story Elements-Plot

Directions: In "January," Bandit's family gets a letter from her father. This sets off a series of events ending in Bandit getting a new American name. Write the main events in chronological order in the boxes below.

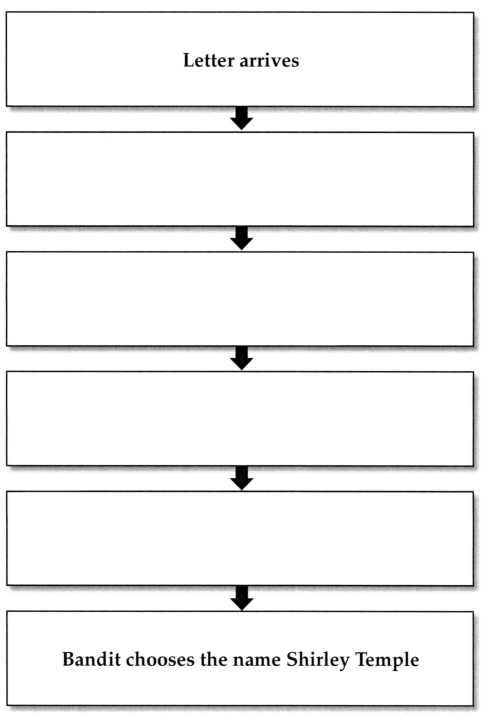

Letter arrives

Bandit chooses the name Shirley Temple

Name _____ Date _____

Story Elements-Character

Directions: Character webs help organize information about a character from a novel. Different parts of the web can be used to describe how the character acts or feels, how the character looks, when or where the character lives, and how others feel about the character. Use the character web below to organize the information about Bandit.

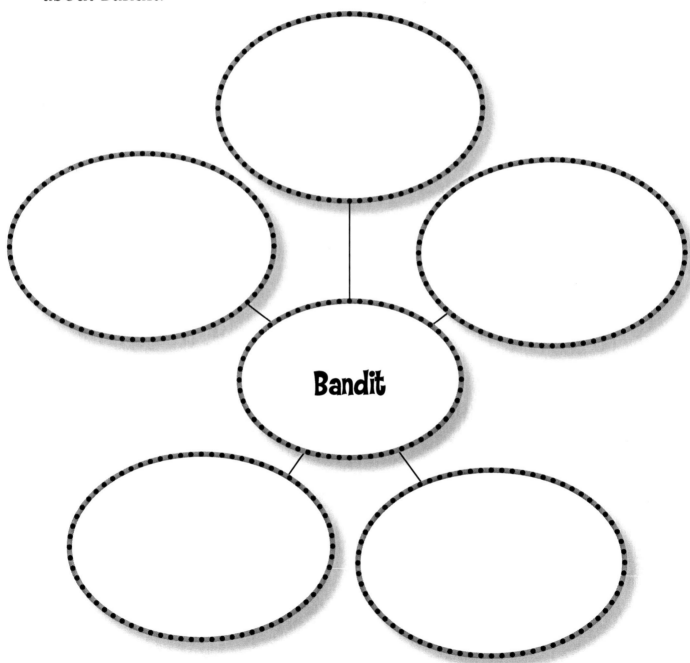

Vocabulary Overview

Key words and phrases from this section are provided below with definitions and sentences about how the words are used in the story. Introduce and discuss these important vocabulary words with students. If you think these words or other words in the story warrant more time devoted to them, there are suggestions in the introduction for other vocabulary activities (page 5).

Word	Definition	Sentence about Text
faltered (February)	felt doubt about doing something	Mother never **falters** during the long journey to America.
unperturbed (February)	calm and relaxed; not upset or worried	Mother is **unperturbed** by the rocking boat or the uncertainty of the journey, but Shirley feels sick and unsure.
torrential (February)	outpouring	There's a **torrential** rain when Mother finds a taxi.
embracing (February)	holding someone in your arms as a way of expressing love or friendship	Shirley runs up to Father, **embracing** him.
ogled (February)	looked at something in a way that suggests strong interest or desire	Shirley **ogles** the tall buildings of the new city.
rebuke (February)	to speak in an angry or critical way	Shirley's father does not **rebuke** her for getting lost.
ambassador (March)	a person who travels to places to promote friendship and goodwill	Mother tells Shirley that she is China's little **ambassador**.
escapade (March)	an exciting, foolish, or dangerous experience or adventure	Shirley does not want her teacher to find out about her lunchtime **escapade**.
eagerly (April)	very excitedly and interestedly	Shirley nods **eagerly** when Joseph invites her to join the kids' baseball game.
content (April)	pleased or satisfied	The bird is **content** as he listens to the melody from the piano.

Vocabulary Activity

Directions: Write four sentences about the story. Use at least one word from the story in each sentence.

Words from the Story

faltered	unperturbed	embracing	ogled	rebuke
ambassador	escapade	eagerly	torrential	content

1. _____

   _____

2. _____

   _____

3. _____

   _____

4. _____

   _____

Directions: Answer this question.

5. Why doesn't Shirley want Mrs. Rappaport to know about her **escapade**?

   _____

   _____

Analyzing the Literature

Provided below are discussion questions you can use in small groups, with the whole class, or for written assignments. Each question is written at two levels so that you can choose the right question for each group of students. For each question, a few key points are provided for your reference as you discuss the book with students.

Story Element	Level 1	Level 2	Key Discussion Points
Setting	How does the author describe the new apartment?	How does the setting influence Shirley's life? Give details in your explanation.	The apartment is small, "barely larger than her own room had been in the clan compound." It is on the third floor of a building that looks like all the others. There is no garden, but there is a kitchen with an icebox and a washing machine. The apartment influences Shirley's life because everything is new to her. She and her mother don't understand how the new appliances work. Shirley must make her way and learn to adjust to this new place.
Character	Describe Father's actions as he shows Shirley and Mother around the apartment.	What do Father's actions reveal as he is showing off the apartment?	Father is excited and proud to show off the new apartment. He knows that it is different from their previous home and explains that they don't have a cook or housekeeper and will need to learn to do these things themselves. He enjoys watching Shirley and Mother figure out these new machines and laughs at their reactions. He is looking forward to witnessing them experience their new home and life.
Plot	How do the events in "March" affect Shirley?	Describe the events in "March." How do they affect Shirley's character development? Provide examples from the text.	Shirley and her mother sign Shirley up for school. She is put in a grade that is for kids older than her because of the difference in how age is calculated in China and America. Shirley is smaller than the other kids and doesn't understand much of what is being said to her. At lunch, the kids take her to a store instead of going to the cafeteria. She eats and enjoys some new foods but feels guilty about it when she gets back. Shirley hopes her teacher and mother do not find out about it. Shirley is enjoying many of the new experiences even though they are challenging.

Name _____ Date _____

Reader Response

Think

Shirley has a hard time making new friends because she can't skate or play baseball, and she often isn't included in other kids' games. Think about a time when you felt left out.

Narrative Writing Prompt

Describe a time when you were left out. How did you feel? Did someone help you?

_____

_____

_____

_____

_____

_____

_____

_____

_____

_____

Name _____ Date _____

Guided Close Reading

Closely reread the section of "March" where Shirley spends her first day at school. Begin with, "Alone, the school mistress and Shirley looked at each other." Stop with, "She thinks there is something wrong with your eyes."

Directions: Think about these questions. In the space below, write ideas as you think. Be ready to share your answers.

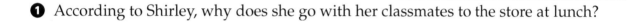

❶ According to Shirley, why does she go with her classmates to the store at lunch?

❷ Use details from the book to describe Shirley's first day of school.

❸ Why does Shirley's teacher write a note to her parents to tell them there is something wrong with Shirley's eyes?

Name _____ Date _____

Making Connections–Mapping
Your Neighborhood

Directions: Draw a detailed map of your neighborhood. Make sure to include local points of interest such as parks, markets, the post office, and other important places. Include a title, symbols, a map key to show what the symbols represent, and a compass rose.

Name _____ Date _____

Language Learning–Figurative Language

Directions: This book is full of sensory details. Read through this section of the book, and list sensory details on the chart below. A couple have already been done for you.

Sense	Example 1	Example 2
sight	Mother "snaked her way through the crowd of travelers."	
smell		
touch	"Out in the sunlight, the air was balmy."	

Name _____ Date _____

Story Elements–Setting

Directions: Think about some of the settings in this section of the book. List four settings. Then, write three details about each of them.

Setting	Details
	• • •
	• • •
	• • •
	• • •

Story Elements–Character

Directions: Pick a character from the book, and write a poem about the character using details from the book. Use the diagram to help you write your poem.

Father	Joseph	Señora Rodriguez
Mother	Toscanini	Mrs. Rappaport

_____
name of character

_____   _____
2 words describing the character

_____   _____   _____
3 words describing a setting that includes the character

_____   _____   _____   _____
4 words describing an event in the story that involves the character

_____
repeat the name of character

Teacher Plans

Vocabulary Overview

Key words and phrases from this section are provided below with definitions and sentences about how the words are used in the story. Introduce and discuss these important vocabulary words with students. If you think these words or other words in the story warrant more time devoted to them, there are suggestions in the introduction for other vocabulary activities (page 5).

Word	Definition	Sentence about Text
collided (May)	hit something or someone with strong force; crashed together or crashed into something	As Shirley crosses the field after school, she **collides** with a runner from the baseball game.
interrogate (May)	to ask someone questions in a thorough and often forceful way	Although the officer tries to **interrogate** Shirley, she does not tell anyone what happened.
persuasive (May)	able to cause people to do or believe something	Mabel is very **persuasive**.
propel (May)	to push or drive (someone or something) forward in a particular direction	Mabel shows Shirley how to **propel** herself on the roller skates.
beckoned (June)	signaled or summoned	The bell **beckons** the kids to their homerooms.
uttered (June)	said	Shirley doesn't understand why the kids laugh after she **utters** Jackie Robinson's name.
injustice (June)	unfair treatment; to treat someone in an unfair way	Mrs. Rappaport tells about Jackie Robinson joining the major leagues despite the **injustice** he faced growing up.
eerie (July)	strange or mysterious	The playground looks **eerie** without kids playing stickball.
emanated (July)	to come out from a source	Shirley's parents don't like the noise that **emanates** from the radio during Dodger games.
sultry (July)	very hot and humid	Even though it is a **sultry** afternoon, Shirley offers to take Toscanini for a walk.

Vocabulary Activity

Directions: Match each word on the left with a synonym, or word that means the same, on the right. Draw lines to match the words. You might need a dictionary to help you.

Word from the Story   Synonyms

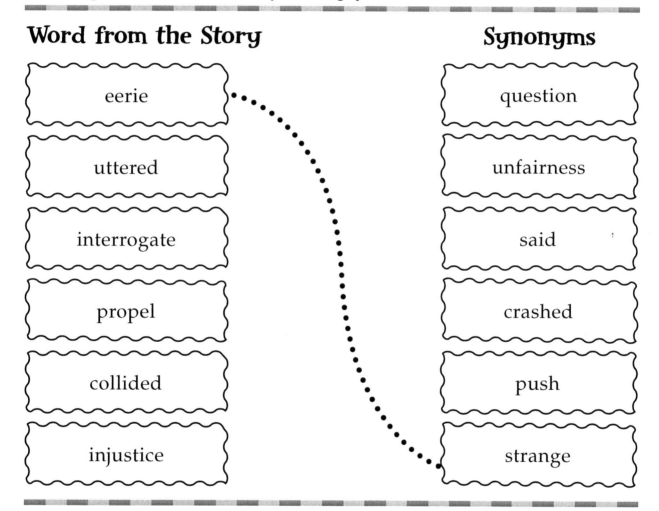

Word from the Story	Synonyms
eerie	question
uttered	unfairness
interrogate	said
propel	crashed
collided	push
injustice	strange

Directions: Answer this question.

1. How is Mabel so **persuasive**? Why do the other children allow Shirley to play stickball?

_____

_____

_____

Teacher Plans

Analyzing the Literature

Provided below are discussion questions you can use in small groups, with the whole class, or for written assignments. Each question is written at two levels so that you can choose the right question for each group of students. For each question, a few key points are provided for your reference as you discuss the book with students.

Story Element	Level 1	Level 2	Key Discussion Points
Character	Who is Shirley's first friend? How do they become friends?	Mabel and Shirley become friends in an odd way. Why does Mabel decide that Shirley is a friend?	Mabel punches Shirley because she interferes in the game. Shirley doesn't hit her back nor does she tell on her, even after her parents take her to the police station. After a few days of being absent from school, Shirley meets Mabel in the morning. Mabel takes Shirley under her wing, and teaches her to play stickball, and to roller skate. She insists that the other kids let Shirley play with them.
Plot	What is the author's message in "July"? How does it help you understand Shirley's point of view?	What is the author's purpose in writing "July"? Cite examples from the text.	The main idea of the chapter is how hard it is for families to be separated. Señora is sad because she has been separated from her daughter for many years and misses her very much. Shirley also misses her extended family, and though she is acclimating to America, she feels as though she is forgetting some of the important things about being Chinese.
Plot	How is Mabel's friendship a turning point in the plot?	What is the significance of Mabel's friendship? How does it influence the events in the other chapters?	Once Mabel and Shirley become friends, the other kids accept Shirley. She learns, through Mabel, how to do many American things and even gets the nickname Jackie Robinson. Shirley is no longer treated as an outsider but as another kid. This influences the plot because other events revolve around her being accepted by the group and learning American customs and culture, such as baseball.

Reader Response

Think

Mabel enters Shirley's life as a bully. Later, they become good friends. Think about Mabel's personality and traits as a friend.

Opinion Writing Prompt

Would you want to be friends with Mabel? Explain why or why not. Use examples from the text to support your answer.

_____

_____

_____

_____

_____

_____

_____

_____

_____

_____

_____

Name _____ Date _____

Guided Close Reading

Closely reread the section of "June" that begins with, "Who's the girl Jackie Robinson?" Stop with, "She felt as if she had the power of ten tigers, as if she had grown as tall as the Statue of Liberty."

Directions: Think about these questions. In the space below, write ideas as you think. Be ready to share your answers.

❶ How does Mrs. Rappaport feel about Jackie Robinson? How do you know? Use words from the text.

❷ How does the author use figurative language to tell about how Shirley is feeling in the last paragraph?

❸ How would this text differ if it were told from the first-person point of view? Explain.

Making Connections–Kinetic Energy

Directions: Shirley gets walked to first base and is able to score after Mabel "sent the ball flying." Mabel is able to do this thanks to kinetic energy. Read the text and respond to the questions.

⋯⋯⋯⋯⋯⋯⋯⋯⋯⋯⋯⋯⋯⋯⋯⋯⋯⋯⋯⋯⋯⋯⋯⋯

Kinetic energy is the energy of motion. Anything that moves has kinetic energy. The kinetic energy of an object depends on its mass. This means that a larger moving object has more energy than a smaller moving object. Kinetic energy also depends on an object's velocity. That is how fast it's moving. This means that an object moving quickly has more energy than a slower object. Kinetic energy can be transferred when objects collide. This can be seen during a game of baseball. First, the pitcher winds up and throws the ball. The pitcher has just transferred the energy from his arm to the ball. Then the batter hits the ball with a bat. Kinetic energy transfers from the bat to the ball. All of that kinetic energy can sometimes shatter the bat!

⋯⋯⋯⋯⋯⋯⋯⋯⋯⋯⋯⋯⋯⋯⋯⋯⋯⋯⋯⋯⋯⋯⋯⋯

1. Explain your understanding of kinetic energy. How does the text support this understanding?

   _____

   _____

   _____

   _____

2. How does the baseball example support the main idea of the text?

   _____

   _____

   _____

Name _____   Date _____

Language Learning–Figurative Language

Directions: Bette Bao Lord uses metaphors to help the reader understand Shirley's experiences as a new immigrant. They help readers form pictures in their minds. Circle the metaphors in the sentences. Then, write what message Lord was trying to convey.

Language Hints!

- A metaphor is a figure of speech. It makes a comparison between two things that are unrelated but share some common characteristics.
- A metaphor is different from a simile. It implies the person, place, action or things is something else without using like or as.

1. "On all sides there was trouble. Mother stood to her right, Father to her left. Behind her, Mabel sat on a garbage can, watching her every move. In front of her, the monster of a building with iron bars." What does this mean?

    _____

    _____

    _____

2. "Mabel, riding on the handrail, whizzed by and blocked her progress on the first landing." What does this mean?

    _____

    _____

    _____

Story Elements–Plot

Directions: Based on the events in this section of the novel, fill in the columns of this graphic organizer.

Somebody wants ...	But ...	So ...
Mabel wants to yell and fight.		
Shirley's parents want to know what happened to her face.		
	The students laugh at Shirley's question.	
		Shirley tells Señora that her parents can watch the apartment house.

Story Elements-Setting

Directions: Reread the section of "July" when Shirley thinks about how she would spend summers in China and think about the details from the text about Brooklyn. Compare and contrast the summer in three different places: Shirley's family home in China, Shirley's home in Brooklyn, and your home. Use the diagram below to help you organize your thoughts.

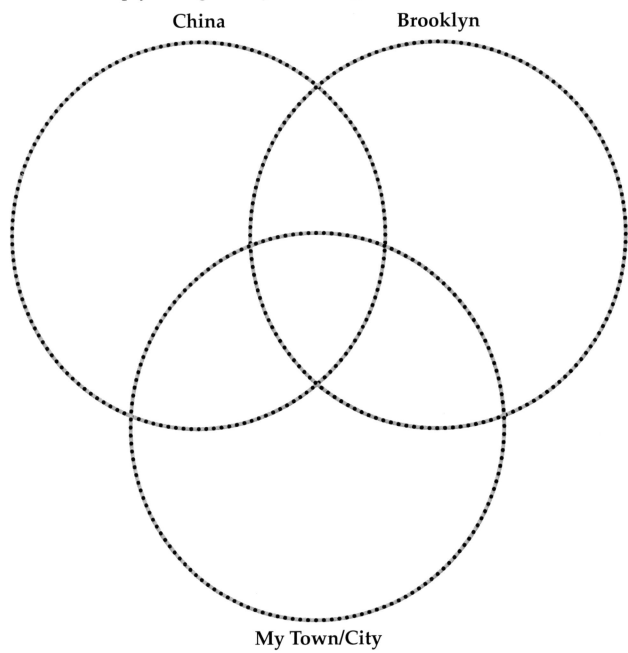

China   Brooklyn

My Town/City

Vocabulary Overview

Key words and phrases from this section are provided below with definitions and sentences about how the words are used in the story. Introduce and discuss these important vocabulary words with students. If you think these words or other words in the story warrant more time devoted to them, there are suggestions in the introduction for other vocabulary activities (page 5).

Word	Definition	Sentence about Text
dimly (August)	having a limited or an insufficient amount of light	The basement of the building is full of strange noises and is **dimly** lit.
murky (August)	very dark or foggy	One corner of the basement is puddled with **murky** water.
ingenuity (August)	skill or cleverness that allows someone to solve problems or invent things	Through his **ingenuity**, Father is able to turn the junk into gifts for the other tenants.
meticulous (August)	very careful about doing something in an extremely accurate and exact way	Father does not let Shirley help with the painting because he is **meticulous** and wants it done well.
venture (September)	to go somewhere that is unknown or dangerous	In her dream, Shirley is afraid to **venture** down a path and get lost.
weary (September)	lacking strength, energy, or freshness	Shirley feels **weary** after struggling to get the triplets' pajamas on and getting them in bed.
clinched (September)	made something certain or final	The triplets unplugged the radio, causing Shirley to miss the Dodgers **clinch** the pennant.
berserk (October)	to become very excited	Everyone goes **berserk** when the Dodgers win the National League.
phenomenon (October)	someone or something that is very impressive or popular especially because of an unusual ability or quality	It is a **phenomenon** that the Yankee pitcher may be the first person to throw a no hitter during the World Series.
banished (October)	to cause something to go away; to get rid of something	Gionfriddo's amazing catch **banishes** all unkind thoughts from Shirley's mind.

Name _____ Date _____

Vocabulary Activity

Directions: Match each word on the left with an antonym on the right. Draw lines to match the words. You might need a dictionary to help you.

Word from the Story	Antonyms
1. banished	careless
2. berserk	calm
3. meticulous	ultra bright
4. murky	let go
5. ingenuity	unoriginal
6. dimly	clear
7. clinched	harbor

Directions: Answer this question.

8. What do the triplets do that causes Shirley to feel **weary**?

_____

_____

_____

Analyzing the Literature

Provided below are discussion questions you can use in small groups, with the whole class, or for written assignments. Each question is written at two levels so that you can choose the right question for each group of students. For each question, a few key points are provided for your reference as you discuss the book with students.

Story Element	Level 1	Level 2	Key Discussion Points
Setting	What impact does the Dodgers being in the World Series have on the setting of the story?	What historical significance does the Dodgers being in the World Series have on the setting of the text?	The fact that the Dodgers win the pennant and play in the World Series is important to the plot. Shirley's summer involves a lot of time inside listening to the games on the radio. Shirley listens to the games while helping her father in the basement, while babysitting, and while she's with her friends at Mr. P's store after school.
Plot	Why does the author describe Shirley's trip to the basement so thoroughly? Use details from the text to answer.	Why does the author focus on the events in the basement after the lights go out? What do you learn about Shirley both during and after?	Shirley's willingness to go down into the basement alone after the lights go out shows that she is brave. She doesn't turn around after the candle gets blown out and continues until her father comes to assist her. She doesn't give up even though the walls feel like blood, and she gets lost. The interaction between Shirley and her father shows mutual respect. He doesn't act like he is saving her, and she acknowledges that she couldn't have done it without him.
Character	What does the secret between Emily and Shirley reveal about each of their characters?	What does the author want the reader to understand about the relationship between Emily and Shirley?	The author wants the reader to understand that the girls have a deep friendship. They get to know each other quickly and become very good friends. Emily gets Shirley to agree to keep a secret about the book, and Shirley doesn't want to hurt her friends' feelings, so she pretends the book and its pictures are more interesting than she thinks they are. Also, Emily shares her lunch with Shirley so Shirley can pay back the money taken from the piggy bank. This shows that the two girls are willing to help each other and have each other's backs.

Name _____ Date _____

Reader Response

Think

Shirley's father uses his ingenuity and salvaged items from the basement to make gifts for each of the tenants. Think about a gift you have given to someone that was a perfect match for them.

Narrative Writing Prompt

Write about why the gifts were perfect for the building tenants. Then, write about a gift you have given someone that was also a perfect fit.

_____

_____

_____

_____

_____

_____

_____

_____

Guided Close Reading

Closely reread from the beginning of "September." Stop with, "My daughter, I'd know each hair on your head."

Directions: Think about these questions. In the space below, write ideas as you think. Be ready to share your answers.

❶ Summarize the central idea of this section of text. Which key details from the text support this central idea?

❷ Consider how the author introduces the idea of the dream sequence. Why does the author choose to use this text structure? Provide evidence from the text.

❸ How does the author use imagery in the text? How does the imagery help you to understand the text? Give examples.

Making Connections–All Out Baseball

Directions: Read about a fun version of baseball called "All Out Baseball." Then, answer the question.

Materials Needed
- three bases and a home plate
- box or bucket of 4–6 various balls (a kickball, a wiffle ball, a soft football, etc.)

How to Play

⚾ Arrange the bases like they would be for a game of baseball. Place the box or bucket of balls near the home plate.

⚾ Divide into two even teams.

⚾ Have the defense take positions in the infield and outfield. The offense forms a line off the field to indicate batting order.

⚾ The first batter takes the equipment out of the box or bucket, one at a time, and throws each ball onto the field.

⚾ The defense is not allowed to move until the final ball is in the air. The batter now runs the bases nonstop and tries to score before the defense can return all the equipment back to the box or bucket.

⚾ Each person on offense gets one turn. Then, the teams switch places to give the other team a turn to score.

1. How does this game compare to a professional baseball game like the ones Shirley listens to?

_____

_____

Language Learning–Proverbs

Directions: Shirley recalls a number of proverbs, or sayings, used by her elders such as "money did not rain from the skies." Pick a proverb from the chart below. Then, draw a picture to represent the wisdom or advice being given.

Language Hints!

- Proverbs are short, popular sayings that are meant to convey advice or wisdom.
- Proverbs are often tied to culture and act as "folk wisdom" to share values.

Proverb	Meaning
look before you leap	think about the consequences before you act
don't count your chickens before they hatch	don't count on something before it happens
birds of a feather flock together	people with similar interests, likes, and appearances hang out together

Name _____ Date _____

Story Elements–Plot

Directions: Select a chapter from this section of the book and review the text. Then, complete the graphic organizer to summarize the plot of that chapter.

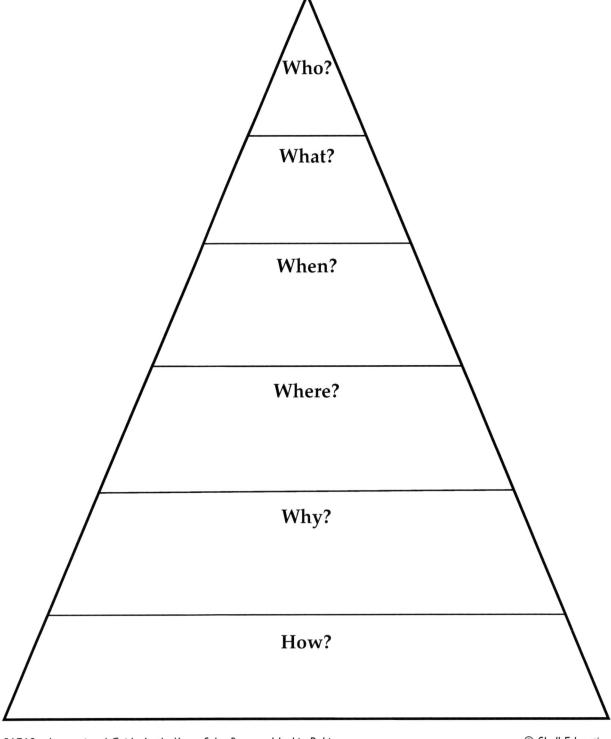

Who?

What?

When?

Where?

Why?

How?

51719—Instructional Guide: In the Year of the Boar and Jackie Robinson

Name _____ Date _____

Story Elements–Character

Directions: In "September," a new student named Emily joins the class. Shirley knows right away that the two of them will be friends. She begins to show Emily around the school and takes her under her wing. Pretend you are Emily. Write about how it feels being a new student and what you think of Shirley befriending you.

_____

_____

_____

_____

_____

_____

_____

_____

_____

_____

_____

_____

Vocabulary Overview

Key words and phrases from this section are provided below with definitions and sentences about how the words are used in the story. Introduce and discuss these important vocabulary words with students. If you think these words or other words in the story warrant more time devoted to them, there are suggestions in the introduction for other vocabulary activities (page 5).

Word	Definition	Sentence about Text
commemorate (November)	to mark by ceremony or observation	Shirley and her family want to **commemorate** the fullest moon of the year but most Americans don't.
elixir (November)	a magical liquid that can cure illness or extend life	Shirley imagines she can see a hare under a cassia tree with the **elixir** of life in its face.
filial (November)	relating to or suitable for a son or daughter	Shirley retold Grandfather's story of the loving bride and the **filial** daughter.
mystified (November)	to be confused or bewildered completely	The parents and the husband are **mystified** to discover the wife and daughter are the same woman.
merged (November)	to be or cause to be combined or blended into a single unit	Walking in from opposite sides of the tree, the women **merge** into one.
juvenile (December)	childish; immature	Emily says Tommy is **juvenile**.
futility (December)	a useless act or gesture	Even though Emily thinks it is an act of **futility**, Shirley is able to convince her to run against Tommy.
ashamed (December)	feeling shame or guilt	Shirley is **ashamed** that Emily wants her to be the class representative.
anticipation (December)	excitement about something that is going to happen	The entire class waits with **anticipation** for the assembly.
eligible (December)	qualified to be chosen; to participate or to receive	Shirley tells Jackie Robinson that she is not **eligible** to become president since she was not born in America.

Name _____ Date _____

Vocabulary Activity

Directions: Fill in the missing words to solve the crossword puzzle.

Words from the Story

commemorate	elixir	mystified	filial	ingenuity
anticipation	futility	ashamed	merged	eligible

Across

2. The family eats moon cakes to _____ the moon.

4. Shirley isn't _____ to be elected president.

6. In grandfather's story, the family was _____ about who was the real girl.

Down

1. Shirley feels _____ that Emily is a better friend than she is.

3. The class can't stand the _____ of waiting for the assembly.

5. The Hare uses a jade mortar to pound the _____ of life.

Analyzing the Literature

Provided below are discussion questions you can use in small groups, with the whole class, or for written assignments. Each question is written at two levels so that you can choose the right question for each group of students. For each question, a few key points are provided for your reference as you discuss the book with students.

Story Element	Level 1	Level 2	Key Discussion Points
Plot	For what reasons do Shirley and her parents forget about the Mid-Autumn Festival?	What is the significance of forgetting the Mid-Autumn Festival?	Shirley and her parents are so wrapped up in their new lives that they completely forget it is coming until they receive moon cakes from Grandfather. It is significant because it shows how their new lives will overshadow their traditions unless they are careful to preserve them.
Character	Why does Shirley want Emily to run for class representative?	What does Emily's run for class representative show about both Emily's and Shirley's characters?	Shirley convinces Emily to run for class representative because they are tired of Tommy's antics. The two girls show ingenuity and determination as they convince their fellow classmates to vote for Emily over Tommy.
Plot	Think of the sequence of events leading up to the assembly. Why does the author choose this order?	How does the author use the sequence of events to show the significance of Emily giving her spot to Shirley?	The author shows how hard Emily and Shirley have to work to defeat Tommy as class representative. Then, when Emily steps down for Shirley to take her place at the assembly, the class eagerly shows how respected Shirley is among her peers. Mabel even makes up a chant to show both girls are appreciated.
Setting	Explain the setting of the assembly. What is special?	What is the significance of the setting of the assembly?	The assembly takes place at the school. The room is decorated with snowflakes, garland, paintings, and a Christmas tree. The Christmas tree sparks Shirley's memory of trimming her very first tree with her parents. It is significant because it allows a flashback to let the reader know that Shirley's mother is pregnant.

Name _____ Date _____

Reader Response

Think

Shirley is anxious as she anticipates meeting Jackie Robinson. Think about a time you were anxious as you waited for something big or important to happen.

Informative/Explanatory Writing Prompt

Tell about a time when you were afraid or nervous about something. Explain why you were feeling the way you were and what steps you took to feel better.

_____

_____

_____

_____

_____

_____

_____

_____

_____

Name _____ Date _____

Guided Close Reading

Closely reread the last section of "December" where Shirley presents the key to Jackie Robinson. Begin with, "Poised between laughter and tears…." Stop at the end of the chapter.

Directions: Think about these questions. In the space below, write ideas or draw pictures as you think. Be ready to share your answers.

❶ What are the author's reasons for including the line from the song, "peace, sleep in heavenly peace."

❷ How do the key details about the conversation between Jackie Robinson and Shirley relate to the main idea of the text?

❸ Why do you think the author included the vision of Shirley's extended family in the balcony clapping for her after the bow?

Name _____ Date _____

Making Connections–Phases of the Moon

Directions: In "November," Shirley and her parents celebrate the fullest moon of the year by eating the moon cakes sent by her grandfather in China. Read the passage about the phases of the moon, and answer the questions.

•••

Both Earth and the moon are constantly orbiting and rotating. As they move, humans only see one part of the moon from Earth. As the moon moves, different parts of it are in the sunlight. When we see the side that is in the sun, it is called the full moon. When we see the side that is away from the sun, it is called a new moon. When the moon looks as though a bite has been taken out of it, it is called a crescent. If the crescent of the moon is getting larger each night it is called a waxing crescent. If it is getting smaller, it is a waning crescent. A quarter moon is when it is exactly half lit by the sun.

•••

1. Explain the relationship between the moon phases, Earth, and the sun.

_____

_____

_____

2. Use the text above to label the phases of the moon.

_____   _____   _____   _____

    1   2   3   4

Language Learning–Types of Nouns

Directions: Read each noun below. Decide to which category each noun belongs. Try to add three more nouns from the book to each category.

Language Hints!

- A common noun names a general person, place, or thing.
- A proper noun names a specific noun and has a capital letter.
- An abstract noun names something you can think of but cannot see or touch.

Word Bank

Mid-Autumn Festival	cloud	poetry	key	Mrs. Rappaport
happiness	boat	Shirley	turkey	Mother

Common Nouns	Proper Nouns	Abstract Nouns

Name _____ Date _____

Story Elements–Character

Directions: The story is told in the third person limited point of view. This means that it is told by a narrator who is not part of the story but knows the thoughts and feelings of one character. Choose a scene from this section, and tell it from the perspective of a character other than Shirley.

_____

_____

_____

_____

_____

_____

_____

_____

_____

_____

_____

_____

Story Elements-Plot

Directions: Choose ten important events that take place throughout the story. Write them in order of occurrence in the boxes below. Cut the boxes apart and mix them up. Give them to a friend to put the story back in chronological order.

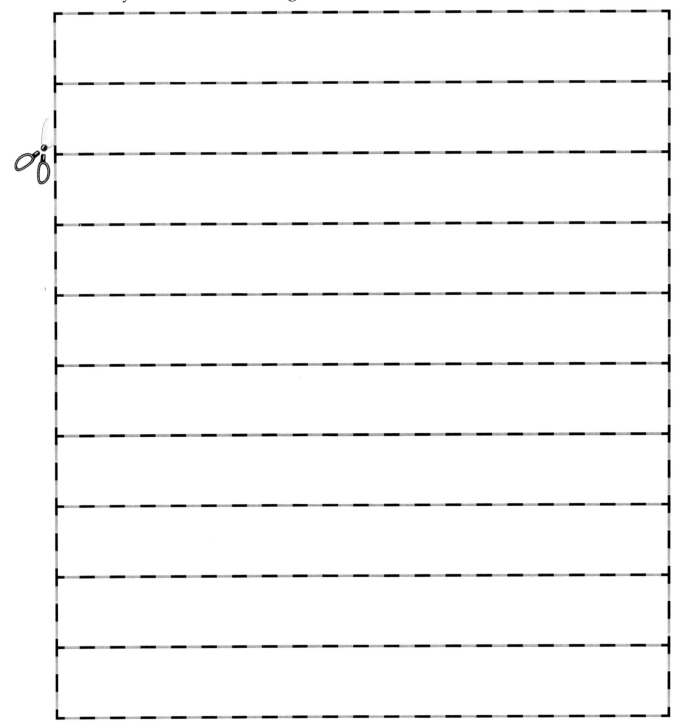

Post-Reading Theme Thoughts

Directions: Choose a main character from *In the Year of the Boar and Jackie Robinson*. Pretend you are that character. Draw a picture of a happy face or a sad face to show how the character would feel about each statement. Then, use words to explain your picture.

Character I Chose _____

Statement	How Do You Feel? 😊 ☹	Explain Your Answer
It is easy to make new friends.		
Learning new things is easy.		
It is important to tell an adult if someone hurts you.		
Good experiences can be bad, and bad experiences can turn out good.		

Name _____ Date _____

Culminating Activity: Americans Who Have Made Differences

Directions: Jackie Robinson, as described by Mrs. Rappaport, is an "American who made a difference." Choose one of the Americans below who has made a difference. Use the Internet and library to gather information about his or her life, what they did, and what is special or unique about his or her story.

Madeline Albright	Thomas Jefferson
Susan B. Anthony	Ervin "Magic" Johnson
Neil Armstrong	Martin Luther King Jr.
Clara Barton	Abraham Lincoln
Alexander Graham Bell	Joe Louis
Daniel Boone	Elijah McCoy
George Washington Carver	Jesse Owens
Cesar Chavez	Rosa Parks
Amelia Earhart	I. M. Pei
Thomas Edison	Eleanor Roosevelt
Henry Ford	Jokichi Takamine
Benjamin Franklin	Harriet Tubman

Culminating Activity: Americans Who Have Made Differences (cont.)

Directions: Use the information you found during your research to complete the graphic organizer. Then, present your findings to your classmates.

Childhood and Early Life

Why is he/she famous? How did he/she make a difference?

Who? _____

Date of Birth: _____

Date of Death: _____

Important Character Traits

Interesting Facts

Culminating Activity: Americans Who Have Made Differences *(cont.)*

Directions: Think about what you have learned about the person you selected. Think about his or her life and accomplishments. Use the space below to jot down your ideas.

Person: _____

What do you think would be different today if this person had not lived?
How does his/her life story help you to better understand a different viewpoint or perspective?
What experiences are similar to or different from your own life?
What character traits does this person have that you wish you had? Why?
What can you do today as a direct result of the person's contributions?

Culminating Activity: Americans
Who Have Made Differences *(cont.)*

Directions: Use the information from the graphic organizer on page 61 and your notes on page 62 to write a 3–5 minute presentation for your class about the person you chose.

_____

_____

_____

_____

_____

_____

_____

_____

_____

_____

_____

Comprehension Assessment

Directions: Fill in the bubble for the best response to each question.

January

1. How do the events in January relate to the theme that each person can make a difference in America?

   Ⓐ They contrast Shirley's life in China with the one she will have in America.

   Ⓑ They demonstrate the importance of customs and family in Shirley's life.

   Ⓒ They help readers to get to know Shirley's character.

   Ⓓ All of the above

February–April

2. Why do Shirley and her mother act so differently when greeting her father?

   Ⓐ Shirley hasn't seen him in a much longer time than her mother.

   Ⓑ Shirley's mother wasn't excited to see him.

   Ⓒ Their relationships with him are different.

   Ⓓ Shirley's mother doesn't want to move to America.

May–July

3. Why, according to Mrs. Rappaport, is baseball fitting as an American sport?

   Ⓐ Each player has the chance to contribute to the team effort.

   Ⓑ It is fast and difficult to learn.

   Ⓒ The pitcher and catcher, like the president and Congress, play more important roles than others.

   Ⓓ It is a game that is enjoyed by American families.

Name _____ Date _____

Comprehension Assessment (cont.)

August–October

4. Explain the events of Shirley's dream and what the dream means.

_____

_____

_____

_____

_____

_____

_____

November–December

5. What does Jackie Robinson say that encourages the students to be the best they can be?

Ⓐ "Do not be pessimistic. Someday, Americans will elect a woman President."

Ⓑ "Thank you, everyone. I shall treasure this day."

Ⓒ "Hooray for the sister of our future President, Shirley Temple Wong."

Ⓓ "For someday you will all hold the keys to making America the greatest country in the world."

Name _____ Date _____

Response to Literature: Favorite Part of the Story

Directions: What is your favorite part of *In the Year of the Boar and Jackie Robinson*? Draw a picture of your favorite scene, and write at least three sentences describing it. Then, answer the questions on page 67 about that scene. Use color and be neat!

_____

_____

_____

_____

_____

_____

Response to Literature:
Favorite Part of the Story *(cont.)*

1. What is happening in this scene? What makes it special and/or relatable?

_____

_____

_____

2. What message does this part of the story communicate, and how does it relate to the main idea or theme?

_____

_____

_____

3. What do you learn about Shirley or another character during this part of the story? Why is this important or significant?

_____

_____

4. How does this scene affect the rest of the book?

_____

_____

Name _____ Date _____

Response to Literature Rubric

Directions: Use this rubric to evaluate student responses.

Great Job	Good Work	Keep Trying
☐ You answered all four questions completely. You included many details.	☐ You answered all four questions.	☐ You did not answer all four questions.
☐ Your handwriting is very neat. There are no spelling errors.	☐ Your handwriting can be neater. There are some spelling errors.	☐ Your handwriting is not very neat. There are many spelling errors.
☐ Your picture is neat and fully colored.	☐ Your picture is neat and some of it is colored.	☐ Your picture is not very neat and/or fully colored.
☐ Creativity is clear in both the picture and the writing.	☐ Creativity is clear in either the picture or the writing.	☐ There is not much creativity in either the picture or the writing.

Teacher Comments: _____

_____

_____

_____

Name _____ Date _____

_____

_____

_____

_____

_____

_____

_____

_____

_____

_____

_____

_____

_____

Answer Key

The responses provided here are just examples of what the students may answer. Many accurate responses are possible for the questions throughout this unit.

Vocabulary Activity—Section 1:
January (page 15)

Illustrations should include ideas and connections to help students know and remember the words.

Guided Close Reading—Section 1:
January (page 18)

1. The author wants readers to understand that there are many traditions and customs surrounding the New Year holiday in China. For example, no one slept because, "a bad dream on any New Year's Eve was an omen of bad tomorrows." Some of the traditions and customs are different than the rest of the year because on, "New Year's Eve, exceptions were the rule."

2. "Bandit jumped to her feet and obeyed" when Grandfather called her. She does this because Grandfather is the "Patriarch of the clan." Bandit jumps up to show respect because she is younger. Bandit's response and Grandfather's reaction by cracking a joke show that Grandfather loves his granddaughter.

3. Although Grand-grand Uncle and his wife are married, they do not address each other because of a long-standing grudge. Bandit acts as a go-between by pleasing both of them. This shows that she knows how to get along with others and knows how to please her elders

Language Learning—Section 1:
January (page 20)

The following parts of the sentences should be circled.

1. Precious Coins; a dumpling

2. holiday banners; glass pieces of a kaleidoscope

3. Bandit's face; a fried lobster

Students should have two or more examples of similes from the book.

Story Elements—Section 1:
January (page 21)

Answers should include major events from the chapter such as: Bandit breaks the vase; She is summoned by Grandmother; She takes Precious Coins with her; She finds out she is moving; The family celebrates the New Year.

Vocabulary Activity—Section 2:
February–April (page 24)

Shirley doesn't want Mrs. Rappaport to find out about her **escapade** because she does not want to lose her ambassadorship.

Guided Close Reading—Section 2:
February–April (page 27)

1. Shirley goes with her classmates because they are her new friends, and she feels like she doesn't have much of a choice.

2. Shirley's first day of school is an adventure. Her teacher reminds her of a cardinal. She sneaks out of school and eats the best food she has ever had. She tries to learn to wink but feels guilty about doing something she shouldn't. She is scared to give her parents the teacher's letter.

3. Mrs. Rappaport thinks there is something wrong with Shirley's eyes because she is blinking with both eyes rather than winking with one. Shirley does this, though, because it is something she learned from the principal as a gesture to show friendliness.

Making Connections—Section 2:
February–April (page 28)

Maps should include important places, symbols, a key, and a compass rose.

Vocabulary Activity—Section 3:
May–July (page 33)

- eerie—strange
- uttered—said
- interrogate—question
- beckoned—summoned
- propel—push
- collided—crashed
- injustice—unfairness

1. Mabel is **persuasive** by intimidating the other kids. She calls them names. The other children allow Shirley to play because they do not want to upset Mabel.

Guided Close Reading—Section 3:
May–July (page 36)

1. Mrs. Rappaport feels as though Jackie Robinson has changed America because he has fought to become successful. She says, "Jackie Robinson is making a difference" and tells the kids that they can make a difference, too, because "no matter what his race, religion or creed...He has the right to speak his mind, to live as he wishes within the law, to elect our officials and stand for office, to excel."

2. The author says that Shirley feels "as if she had the power of ten tigers" and "as if she had grown as tall as the Statue of Liberty" to explain how Shirley feels after figuring out why her father brought her to America. She feels wise and that she has been given an opportunity to become the best she can be in America.

3. The text would differ because the reader wouldn't be able to have an objective interpretation of the events that are occurring but would only be able to understand Shirley's side or perspective. The third-person narrator helps the reader understand the context of what Shirley is experiencing in a way that another point of view would not.

Making Connections—Section 3:
May–July (page 37)

1. Kinetic energy is the energy of motion. The text supports this understanding because it says, "anything that moves has kinetic energy."

2. The example of baseball supports the main idea of the text because it illustrates when we see kinetic energy in common activities.

Language Learning—Section 3:
May–July (page 38)

1. Circle: "monster of a building"; The building was gigantic and scary.

2. Circle: Mabel, riding on the handrail, whizzed by"; She flew by quickly like a bee.

Story Elements—Section 3:
May–July (page 39)

Somebody wants…	But…	So…
Mabel wants to yell and fight.	Shirley stands her ground.	Mabel punches Shirley in both eyes.
Shirley's parents want to know what happened to her face.	She will not tell them and doesn't want to be a tattletale.	Shirley and Mabel become friends.
Shirley wants to know why the other kids call her Jackie Robinson.	The students laugh at Shirley's question.	Mrs. Rappaport asks Mabel to explain the connection.
Señora wants to visit her Nonnie.	She cannot leave the apartment house unattended.	Shirley tells Señora that her parents can watch the apartment house.

Vocabulary Activity—Section 4:
August–October (page 42)

1. banished; harbor

2. berserk; calm

3. meticulous; careless

4. murky; clear

5. ingenuity; unoriginal

6. dimly; ultra bright

7. clinched; let go

8. The triplets shout that they want to sit in a specific chair, they spit out food, tug at Shirley's skirt, and keep yelling "Hooray!"

Guided Close Reading—Section 4:
August–October (page 45)

1. Shirley is worried that she is changing too much and that her family in China would no longer recognize her because she is too American. She has a dream in which they circle her and laugh. The neighbors are also telling her how much she has grown up. She wants to stay true to her Chinese heritage. When she wakes, she asks her mother if she would still know her. Her mother assures her that she is still the same person and that she would always know every hair on Shirley's head.

2. The author introduces the idea that Shirley has changed prior to the dream sequence. Then, the author makes it clear to the reader that Shirley is dreaming when the text states, "Yawning, she closed her eyes. When she opened them she was in Chungking." The author chooses this structure to show how Shirley thinks her relatives in China would think differently than her friends and family in America.

3. The author uses imagery to give the reader a mental image of what Shirley is going through and to paint a picture of what is going on. When the text describes how Shirley's "legs feel heavy, as if she was wading through deep water," or when she runs into the wall and "she could see over it, but it was too high for her to scale," the reader gets a sense of being there with Shirley.

Vocabulary Activity—Section 5: November–December (page 51)

Across:	Down:
2. commemorate	1. ashamed
4. eligible	3. anticipation
6. mystified	5. elixir

Guided Close Reading—Section 5: November–December (page 54)

1. The line from the song reminds readers of the setting. Shirley and Jackie Robinson are on stage at a school Christmas performance. There is an audience, and the other kids are singing. The line also reminds the reader that the world in 1947 is becoming a peaceful place where Americans are given an opportunity to be the best they can be.

2. Jackie Robinson's speech tells about the importance of each person and how everyone "holds the key to making America the greatest country in the world." He also demonstrates this when he talks to Shirley and insists she can be President of the United States until she explains she isn't eligible. These relate to the main idea of the text because each person in America brings his or her own history and understanding, and that is what makes America great.

3. Possible answer includes: I think Bette Bao Lord includes the vision of Shirley's extended family from China to show that they would be proud of the person she has become in America. Prior to Shirley leaving, they are worried for her and don't understand why her father wanted to move. Additionally, Shirley struggles to find her way as a Chinese American. But by the end of the year, she adjusts to her new life and is proud of the person she has become.

Making Connections—Section 5: November–December (page 55)

1. The light from the sun hits the moon and when the lit side is facing Earth we can see it.

2. New moon; waxing crescent; full moon; waning crescent

Language Learning—Section 5: November–December (page 56)

Common Nouns	Proper Nouns	Abstract Nouns
key	Mid-Autumn Festival	poetry
turkey	Shirley	happiness
boat	Mrs. Rappaport	
cloud		

Comprehension Assessment (pages 64–65)

1. D. All of the above

2. C. Their relationships with him are different.

3. A. Each player has the chance to contribute to the team effort.

4. In the dream, Shirley is walking up the Mountain of Ten Thousand Steps. She comes to a fork in the road and hears her mother and her father calling her, each from different directions. The voices disappear, so she runs in the opposite direction, finding herself trapped by a wall. She sees her cousins and her Grand-grand Uncle. He shows her his painting of Shirley as a bird with green feathers and red palms.

5. H. "For someday you will all hold the keys to making America the greatest country in the world."